MW00877227

Samila Rivera is a writer, avid reader and newly published author located in Lincoln, Rhode Island. Journaling since her young years fueled her passion to create expressive pieces and poetry from personal experiences. Writing a poetry book has been a long-time goal for her and Rise of a Sunflower has made that idea a reality.

Instagram @_concrete_sunflower_

My greatest awakening came from loving and losing.
This is healing, self-awareness, re-discovering love
within myself and everything around me. I hope you
find a little something to help you do the same.

All my love

His insecurities were so deep
He wanted me to live in the boundaries of them
Afraid to speak up
Afraid to seek
On eggshells I walked
He wanted me to please them
I just wanted to be free
This isn't for me to exist within the walls of his defeat
Every time I tried to leave, he told me this was it
Insecurities would die as he would try to see past them
But they were as deep as the sea
He just couldn't see more than the waves against him
I was stuck in the layers of deceit
I caused some of this
So, I stayed
Bound by the odds against us
How can this cycle break?
Can we ever find forgiveness?
But I love him
I'll stay
Hope things will change
The last thing I wanted was to live with regret
But then I realized this is exactly what we were doing
Existing as hostages between love and regret

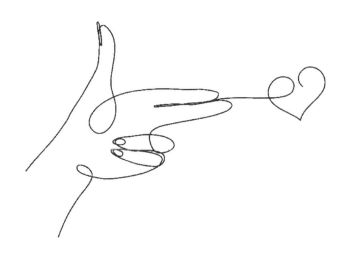

It was hard to get out of bed today
I'm weak
I haven't eaten for a few days
I am not even sure what date it is
My body is barely hanging on
Barely moving
Barely breathing
Barely feeling
Can I just close my eyes until I must wake up again?
Can tomorrow please be better?
Barely moving
Barely breathing
Barely feeling
This isn't living
being barely me

Tears streamed down my face
What are we doing?
Emptiness fills the room
So many silent tears every night
So many words left unsaid
We were so close yet so far
Weight of the pain we carried made larger spaces
between us
What we were now - a distant memory
What we became
just bodies taking up spaces

Repeat:

I release my attachment to whatever doesn't serve me well

It all started with love
You were created with that truly madly deeply kind of love
What we once imagined as impossible became our reality
Eventually all we had left of us was held together by you
Our glue
If you ever ask if there was ever love
I want you to know
Through every difficult road we navigated
Even when we found what was best
All the best
Yes
It all started with love
Truly, Madly, Deeply kind of love

We should have talked more
More uncomfortable conversations
Less uncomfortable silences
Less misunderstanding
More understanding

My heart is going to explode
Let me pick up this pen
What do I have to lose?
my tears fall
transforming into words
Emotions spilling over
weaving into this paper
All this chaos within me
Somehow
Everything is flowing
Hearts pumping slower
This pen isn't stopping
Expressing
Releasing
Free

never thought we would get so comfortable living this
lie
you and I
I am so confused
I really don't know what to do
never wanted to feel so out of control
I feel so helpless
Crazy how much things can change
There was a beautiful beginning to all of this
I guess we were in over our heads
True what they say all good things come to an end
If only we accepted that sooner
Talked more about what was going on inside
Maybe we could have had some more peace
Instead we just went down in flames

I would rather be alone
Me, myself and I
I have been thinking about it a lot
It's Hard to believe
There was a time, I saw no future unless it was with
you
Getting old and grey
perhaps a white picket fence
more kids
maybe even a dog or two
now it's like we can't even look at each other
never mind, say the words I love you
the pain is etched on our chests
we can't manage to get ahead
I realize there is just some people who aren't for you
You aren't for them
Time holds no weight
When you aren't flourishing
Counting how many reasons we should stay
Couldn't come up with many
Still hard not to feel like you're losing
It's like a part of you dies
When the love stops growing

As I looked in the mirror
I didn't see everything he said
I was not or could never be
Instead I saw more, I saw myself clearly
Suddenly through not being enough for him
I realized I was more than enough for me

Repeat:

I am beautiful, resilient and worthy.

The art of letting go doesn't happen overnight. How can people say it just happens? How can we expect that to be possible? When we hold tight grips on things, people and places for so long that equally letting go takes time too. It's sometimes slow, uneasy but consistent and it happens naturally little by little. Don't feel like you must rush your process or feel guilty for working through it.

Trust your process, little by little, bit by bit

No matter how uncomfortable the process can get or how lonely, progress over desires, self-awareness over self-destruction

There is a battlefield going on inside me
Nothing I am doing feels right
Nothing I am saying makes sense
No one knows this is happening
I can't seem to break from this getting down on my
knees to pray is all I have left
My mind keeps telling me I can't get shit right
I feel like I'm losing
Tears are overflowing
I catch a glimpse of myself in the mirror
My vision is blurry
I don't recognize who she is
I have always felt stronger than this
I should have done better taking care of myself
I close my eyes
Take some deep breaths in
I can do this
I can win
This is a storm
I don't have to brave alone
I can't do this alone
I need to reach out
I need some help

There are people who will only focus on the odds that may be against you, then there are those that can see the extent of your will, dedication and capabilities
Those are your people....

My heart has seen better days
Not sure when I will be able to see things the same
This upside-down view has me going insane
I was doing a good job not facing anything
You think your living in peace
Instead your skeletons are just racking up
Waiting for release
Heartbreak it's hard to explain
Shit hits you hard
But for me it was the reality, that I just never fought
So much easier pretending
Damn, I was wrong
Coming face to face with all the times you gave up
Turned a blind eye
Made an excuse
Its crazy how fast and how much we can lose
When we stop choosing ourselves

Repeat:

Peace & Healing are my responsibility and mine only

My thoughts never seem to settle
Analyzing everything
Breaking you, this and that down
Mind full of metaphors
It's exhausting
So, I write
I can hardly catch the words
Good thing this ink dries fast enough
Being like this
It's like my mind is on a new journey
Everyday
Writing always feels like growth
Even if it all started
with what felt like breaking first

You never tried to understand
Instead, constantly bullying me
I'll admit it
You had me tight in your grip for a minute
Your attempt to destroy my strength
Pushed me to the edge
I didn't always say the right things
Made decisions from pain
Trying to fight for what was fair
I was constantly knocked down
So many fears
So much confusion
Struggled to remain true to myself
I have grown past that now
I'm moving differently these days
There's no dragging me around anymore
My battles are selected carefully
Even if that means being misunderstood
Peace and happiness will remain my priority

A person's perception of you is their reality not yours. You are not responsible to make sure other's see the heart behind your actions.

Anyone who is more focused on being against you will never see the best in you

Stay in your light, you know your truth, and that is all That will ever matter.

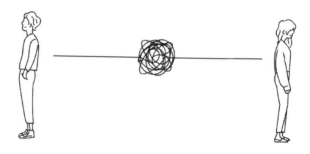

It's been a long time since he's been in front of me
My chest is heavy
I can see his hands are shaking
Still so much chaos between us
I have a lot to say
But I can't find the words
I start to turn around
So, I can walk away
I shouldn't have started this
Never mind I said
Tears start to stream down my face
I looked at him one more time
I managed to say
I am sorry
No explanation
No more pointing fingers
Two wrongs never make it right
In that moment I realized that was all I ever had to say
I just need some healing
I know he does too
I hope today he found some of it
As those three words left my lips
I felt a weight off my chest
His response didn't even matter
I know he's still bitter
I am not even sure he will ever be sorry
But I forgive him
Strongest thing I ever did

While I almost drowned in a sea of my emotions
I had a moment
My conscious reminded me
Take a deep breath
It was like new life was replacing the empty parts of me
I recognize there is still a lot of work to do
I am still healing
But, isn't that the beautifully broken part of my story?
That I am at least on my way

Repeat:
There is nothing stopping me from growing
I know what I want
I know I deserve it

In this moment I reflect
On new beginnings
The first steps I have taken forward
The lesson's I have learned
When my mind tries to play tricks on me
I will choose to celebrate
Honor my progress
Trust my process

There is light all around us
Look for it
When you find it
Follow it
Bask in it
Never lose sight
Even if it storms
No matter how strong the winds or dark the clouds
Storms will pass
The sun will make it's way even if there is just a gap
Keep your face towards it
Just like sunflowers do and the darkness will remain
Behind you

She is multi-layered
Her energy is a rainbow of color
Sweet poetry that rolls right off the tongue
To understand her
It's much deeper than reading the chapters within her

We can so easily cry about the same problem over and over, but we can't seem to find joy over and over. Remaining in the places that confuse us, in the arms of those who hurt us and simply seeing what is going wrong rather than what is going right. You always have a choice and take's effort to see and strength to follow but you can, and I hope you choose to over and over.

There is enough carelessness
I refuse to join
It is my sense of heart
that balances out my world

When the day reaches completion
And we lay our heads down
While there may be war outside our doors
Confusion in what may be truth
What is deception
All that matters
That we remain true in knowing love heals
We are nothing without love
Within us
For humanity
Our dear ones
While the world may be at war
May we remain
Anchored in love

Less forgiveness
Hearts left stagnant
Prisoners to bitterness and anger
Running with the false belief that when you forgive
you're letting that person off easy
Correction,
It is freedom and clarity
Ultimate power move
Forgiveness is for you

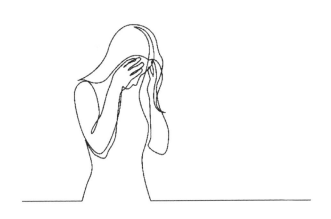

I have struggled to see the fight in me, I have fallen victim to fear, anxiety and depression from the wounds that have tried to weigh me down. Fear that I will start and not finish, settle or allow other's perceptions of me to cloud my vision. We have an obligation to bring the best out of the cards we have been dealt. Emancipate yourself from any mindset of "it is what it is" for we have control over our attitude, energy, effort.

People who love you will never leave room
For you to question their intentions
Ever...

Repeat:
I will be kind and compassionate with my body and soul

Taking the high road isn't always picking and choosing your battles – it also means standing up for yourself even if it's uncomfortable. Never give anyone the foundation to disrespect, control or demean you. You can say no and enough is enough! You may be misunderstood, don't allow that to discourage you. Those who love you know your heart, intentions and character are all that matter and everything else is just noise. Keep building yourself up, celebrate your victories but always remain accountable. Never let anyone get comfortable with hurting you.

Repeat:
Whatever I truly want, I can achieve
No idea of mine is too big or small
Because I am behind it already makes it so damn special

Anti-feelings culture
Seems to be what is happening these days
So many games played
More rules being made
Can't even call first
Apparently, you must wait three days
It is an all ages thing
There is no leading with love
Instead attraction says it all
Forgetting heart and compassion are long lasting
While looks fade
But everyone is still asking for something real,
marriage and kids.
Missing the mark trying to match
#relationshipgoals
Nothing real about it
All smoke and mirrors
Looking for a future?
Look beyond the surface
Look for soul
You're bound to crash and burn
Creating relationships for a hashtag and likes

We all have a deep desire to meet another
Who will gently unravel the many layers of who
we are
To learn
To accept
To understand
And when they find parts of us that are a bit
jaded, confused and dark
That they will stay
And love us anyway

The moments that have brought me to my knees
Tears that could have created oceans
Sleepless nights I replayed every detour and delay
When pieces of me once laid at my feet
I chose to stand
Against my insecurities
Undressing myself of my mistakes and uncertainties
Instead of hiding
This is my truth
I am hurting
I am healing
I am living and breathing
Devoted to uncovering all the magic that I am
I am on the right path
I am ready to release the stories in my head
No longer captive to the past
I am free

Take your time
Not everything
That feels good
Is good for you

Repeat:
I am where I am supposed to be
I have no timeline to reach
I will stay present and let things fall naturally

**S**elf-awareness
**E**mancipation of negativity
**L**earning process
**F**orgiving
**L**iberating
**O**bligation
**V**ulnerable
**E**xactly what you deserve

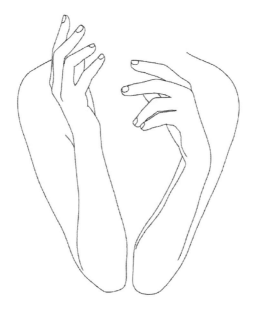

While searching for love and commitment
So many women yelling loud and proud they are
Heartless savages
Walking in the miseries of the past
Focused on just finding a relationship
Before really loving themselves
Setting up the next to fail even at their best
Women grow your roots
Discover the depths of your beauty
Make peace with the past
While you are blooming
Become rooted in a silent strength
You will stand out in the field
Apart from the rest

As easy as you can see the best in him
Don't ignore the rest
He can only pretend for so long
So, believe him
When his true colors show
When the waves he creates
Start crashing into you
Getting higher and stronger
Stop testing his waters
Relationships they may not always easily flow
The storms will come
But I promise you this
The real one will reach down
Bring you back up to the surface
While the wrong one
Baby girl, he will drown you

You are too damn dope to be someone's sometimes
Part-time or in the meantime

I will always be the person who shows up. I won't stop seeing the best in other's and the world, I'll stay soft and kind regardless of the pain I have endured. I'll make sure when you are in my presence you feel heard and seen. Whenever anyone tries to tell you you're not worth it, I will be the first to tell you that you are, the same way I do for myself. I won't stop loving with all the depths of my soul. I found the greatest peace when I discovered these were my strengths and not my weaknesses, I have learned that I can love from afar, boundaries are healthy, and overstepping will never be an option.

For all the time and difficulty, it has taken to rebuild my little universe, peace and happiness. What I have understood most is my scars do not have to become my weapons, bitterness isn't protection, a hardened heart isn't strength. Instead forgiveness is freedom and leading with love in all things is my strength.

58674404R00035

Made in the USA
Middletown, DE
08 August 2019